Ooey-gooey Animals

Jellyfish

Lola Schaefer

Raintree

www.raintreepublishers.co.uk

Visit our website to find out more information about **Raintree** books.

To order:

☎ Phone 44 (0) 1865 888112

🖹 Send a fax to 44 (0) 1865 314091

🖥 Visit the Raintree Bookshop at www.raintreepublishers.co.uk to browse our catalogue and order online.

First published in Great Britain by Raintree, Halley Court, Jordan Hill, Oxford OX2 8EJ, part of Harcourt Education.
Raintree is a registered trademark of Harcourt Education Ltd.

Editorial: Nick Hunter and Diyan Leake
Design: Sue Emerson (HL-US) and Joanna Sapwell
Picture Research: Amor Montes de Oca (HL-US) and Ginny Stroud-Lewis
Production: Lorraine Hicks

Originated by Dot Gradations
Printed and bound in China by South China Printing Company

ISBN 1 844 21021 9 (hardback)
07 06 05 04 03
10 9 8 7 6 5 4 3 2 1

ISBN 1 844 21029 4 (paperback)
08 07 06 05 04
10 9 8 7 6 5 4 3 2 1

British Library Cataloguing in Publication Data

Schaefer, Lola
Jellyfish
593.5'3
A full catalogue record for this book is available from the British Library.

Acknowledgements

The publishers would like to thank the following for permission to reproduce photographs: Corbis pp. **1**, **5**, **6** (Stephen Frink), **8** (W. Wayne Lockwood, MD), **10** (Cordaiy Photo Library Ltd), **12L** (Jeffrey L. Rotman), **14**, **16** (Amos Nachoum), **17** (Brandon D Cole), **23** (gel, Brandon D. Cole; mucus, Cordaiy Photo Library Ltd); HHP p. **13** (Howard Hall); Index Stock Imagery, Inc. pp. **4**, **18**; Karen Gowlett-Holmes p. **20**; Norbert Wu Photography pp. **19**, **21** (Peter Parks/IQ-3D/Mo Yung Productions); Peter Morris p. **12R**; Photovault pp. **7** (Wernher Krutein), **9** (Wernher Krutein), **11** (Wernher Krutein), **15** (Wernher Krutein), **22**, **23** (bell, tentacles, Wernher Krutein), **24**, back cover (both images, Werner Krutein)

Cover photograph of a jellyfish, reproduced with permission of Corbis (Brandon D. Cole)

Every effort has been made to contact copyright holders of any material reproduced in this book. Any omissions will be rectified in subsequent printings if notice is given to the publishers.

 CAUTION: Remind children that it is not a good idea to handle wild animals. Children should wash their hands with soap and water after they touch any animal.

Some words are shown in bold, **like this.** You can find them in the glossary on page 23.

Contents

What are jellyfish?

Jellyfish are animals that live in the sea.

They do not have any bones.

Jellyfish bodies are filled with **gel**.

Gel is clear and watery.

Where do jellyfish live?

Some jellyfish live in cold water.

Some live in warm water.

Jellyfish can live in shallow water close to land.

They can also live in deep water.

What do jellyfish look like?

Some jellyfish come in different colours.

Some jellyfish are see-through.

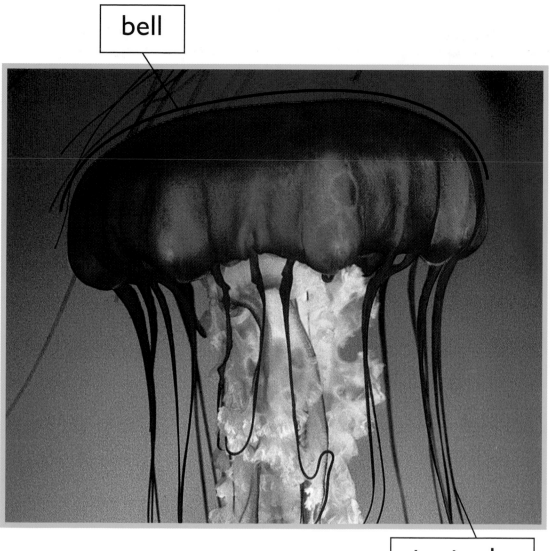

bell

tentacle

Jellyfish bodies are called **bells**.

Tentacles hang from the bell.

What do jellyfish feel like?

Jellyfish feel soft and gooey.

There is **mucus** on their bodies.

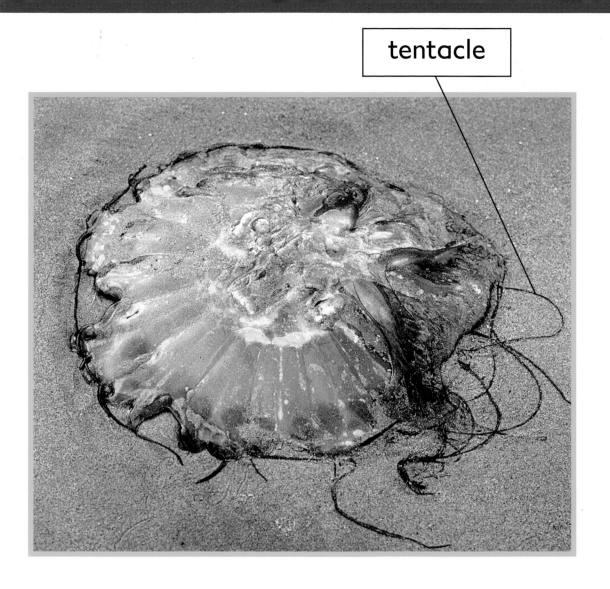

tentacle

It is not a good idea to touch jellyfish.

Some jellyfish **tentacles** can sting!

11

How big are jellyfish?

Some jellyfish **bells** are very big.

Some are as small as a marble.

The **tentacles** on this jellyfish are longer than this diver!

How do jellyfish move?

Jellyfish take water into their **bell**.

Then they push it out again.

This makes them move forward.

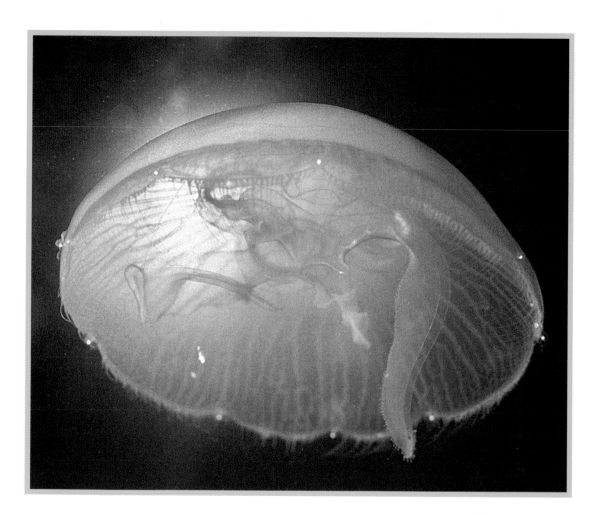

Waves can move jellyfish from place to place in the sea.

What do jellyfish do all day?

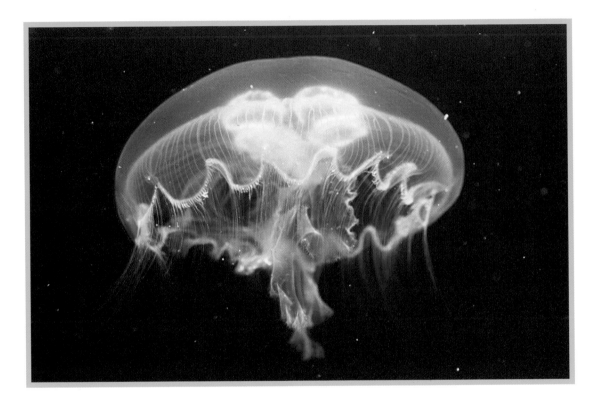

Jellyfish swim through the water.

They are always hunting for food.

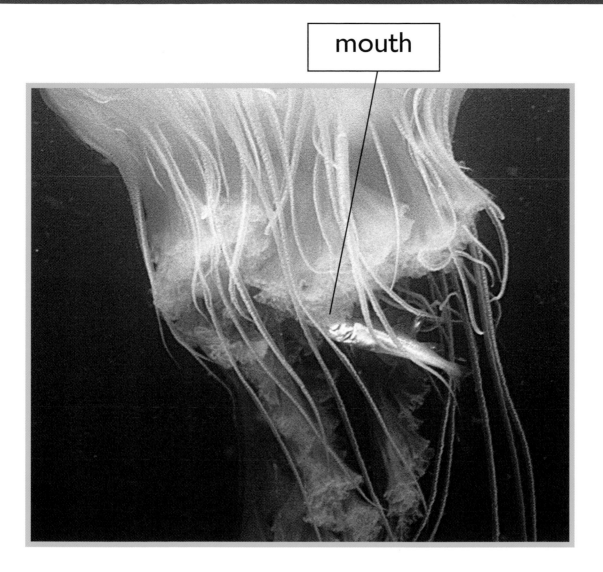

mouth

Jellyfish have a mouth under their **bell**.

They use their **tentacles** to bring food to their mouth.

What do jellyfish eat?

Jellyfish eat other animals in the sea.

They eat small animals and fish.

They sting animals with their **tentacles**.

Then they eat them.

Where do new jellyfish come from?

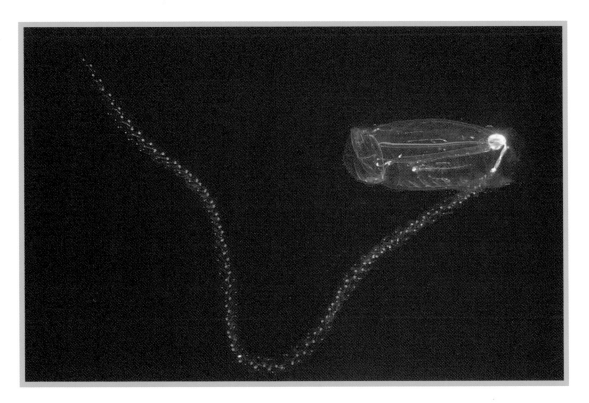

Adult jellyfish lay eggs in the water.

The eggs grow into small animals.

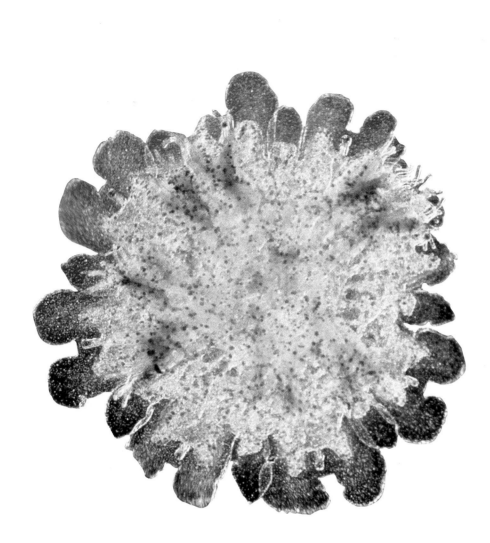

These animals grow round shapes on them.

The round shapes break off and grow into jellyfish.

21

Quiz

What are these jellyfish parts?

Can you find them in the book?

Look for the answers on page 24.

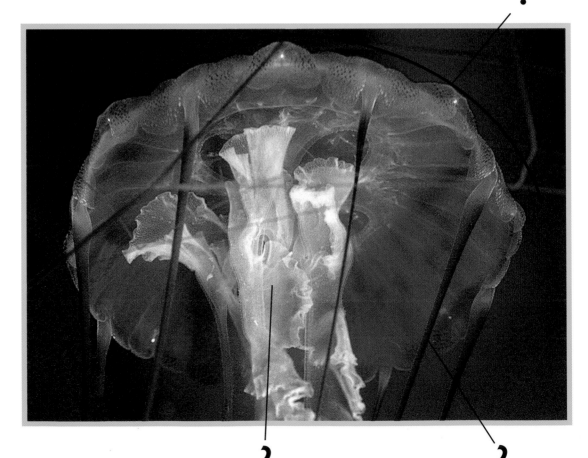

Glossary

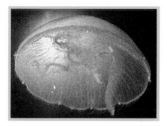

bell
body of a jellyfish

gel
very thick, clear liquid

mucus
slimy stuff that is on or in an animal's body

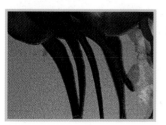

tentacles
long, thin parts that some animals have on their body

Index

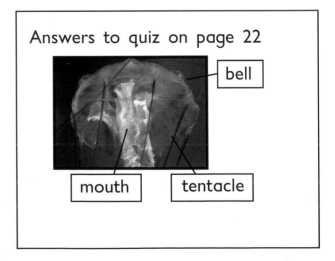

Answers to quiz on page 22

bell

mouth

tentacle